WALK ON!

WHERE THE WALKERS ROAM

BY STACEY LANNIGAN

This book is dedicated to my wonderful Nan, Yvonne Scougal, who has held a passion for walking for as long as I can remember. I hope that you, and other walkers like yourself, use this book to record all your marvellous memories of your travels.

A Walk To Remember

Date: _____

Location: _____

Weather: _____

Company:

_____
_____
_____

Key Memorable Moments:

_____
_____
_____
_____
_____
_____
_____

Write About The Walk:

_____
_____
_____
_____
_____
_____
_____
_____
_____
_____
_____
_____
_____
_____
_____
_____
_____
_____
_____
_____
_____
_____
_____
_____
_____
_____
_____
_____
_____
_____
_____

Rate Your Walk:

Spectacular   Terrible

1   2   3   4   5

Would You Go On This Walk Again & Why?:

_____
_____
_____
_____
_____
_____
_____
_____
_____
_____
_____
_____
_____
_____
_____
_____

A Walk To Remember

Date: _____

Location: _____

Weather: _____

Company:

_____
_____
_____

Key Memorable Moments:

_____
_____
_____
_____
_____
_____
_____

Write About The Walk:

_____
_____
_____
_____
_____
_____
_____
_____
_____
_____
_____
_____
_____
_____
_____
_____
_____
_____
_____
_____
_____
_____
_____
_____
_____
_____
_____
_____
_____
_____

Rate Your Walk:

Spectacular   Terrible

1   2   3   4   5

Would You Go On This Walk Again & Why?:

_____
_____
_____
_____
_____
_____
_____
_____
_____
_____
_____
_____
_____
_____
_____
_____
_____

A Walk To Remember

Date: _____

Location: _____

Weather: _____

Company:

_____
_____
_____

Key Memorable Moments:

_____
_____
_____
_____
_____
_____
_____

Write About The Walk:

_____
_____
_____
_____
_____
_____
_____
_____
_____
_____
_____
_____
_____
_____
_____
_____
_____
_____
_____
_____
_____
_____
_____
_____
_____
_____
_____
_____
_____
_____
_____
_____

Rate Your Walk:

<u>Spectacular</u>   <u>Terrible</u>

1   2   3   4   5

Would You Go On This Walk Again & Why?:

_____
_____
_____
_____
_____
_____
_____
_____
_____
_____
_____
_____
_____
_____
_____
_____
_____

A Walk To Remember

Date: _____

Location: _____

Weather: _____

Company:

_____
_____
_____

Key Memorable Moments:

_____
_____
_____
_____
_____
_____
_____

Write About The Walk:

_____

_____

_____

_____

_____

_____

_____

_____

_____

_____

_____

_____

_____

_____

_____

_____

_____

_____

_____

_____

_____

_____

_____

_____

_____

_____

_____

_____

_____

_____

_____

_____

_____

Rate Your Walk:

<u>Spectacular</u>   <u>Terrible</u>

1   2   3   4   5

Would You Go On This Walk Again & Why?:

_____
_____
_____
_____
_____
_____
_____
_____
_____
_____
_____
_____
_____
_____
_____
_____

A Walk To Remember

Date: _____

Location: _____

Weather: _____

Company:

_____
_____
_____

Key Memorable Moments:

_____
_____
_____
_____
_____
_____
_____

Write About The Walk:

_____
_____
_____
_____
_____
_____
_____
_____
_____
_____
_____
_____
_____
_____
_____
_____
_____
_____
_____
_____
_____
_____
_____
_____
_____
_____
_____
_____
_____
_____
_____

Rate Your Walk:

<u>Spectacular</u>   <u>Terrible</u>

1   2   3   4   5

Would You Go On This Walk Again & Why?:

_____
_____
_____
_____
_____
_____
_____
_____
_____
_____
_____
_____
_____
_____
_____
_____
_____

A Walk To Remember

Date: _____

Location: _____

Weather: _____

Company:

_____
_____
_____

Key Memorable Moments:

_____
_____
_____
_____
_____
_____
_____

Write About The Walk:

_____
_____
_____
_____
_____
_____
_____
_____
_____
_____
_____
_____
_____
_____
_____
_____
_____
_____
_____
_____
_____
_____
_____
_____
_____
_____
_____
_____
_____
_____
_____
_____

Rate Your Walk:

Spectacular   Terrible

1   2   3   4   5

Would You Go On This Walk Again & Why?:

_____
_____
_____
_____
_____
_____
_____
_____
_____
_____
_____
_____
_____
_____
_____
_____

A Walk To Remember

Date: _____

Location: _____

Weather: _____

Company:

_____
_____
_____

Key Memorable Moments:

_____
_____
_____
_____
_____
_____
_____

Write About The Walk:

_____
_____
_____
_____
_____
_____
_____
_____
_____
_____
_____
_____
_____
_____
_____
_____
_____
_____
_____
_____
_____
_____
_____
_____
_____
_____
_____
_____
_____
_____
_____
_____
_____
_____

Rate Your Walk:

Spectacular   Terrible

1   2   3   4   5

Would You Go On This Walk Again & Why?:

_____
_____
_____
_____
_____
_____
_____
_____
_____
_____
_____
_____
_____
_____
_____
_____
_____

A Walk To Remember

Date: _____

Location: _____

Weather: _____

Company:

_____
_____
_____

Key Memorable Moments:

_____
_____
_____
_____
_____
_____
_____

Write About The Walk:

_____

_____

_____

_____

_____

_____

_____

_____

_____

_____

_____

_____

_____

_____

_____

_____

_____

_____

_____

_____

_____

_____

_____

_____

_____

_____

_____

_____

_____

_____

_____

_____

_____

Rate Your Walk:

<u>Spectacular</u>   <u>Terrible</u>

1   2   3   4   5

Would You Go On This Walk Again & Why?:

_____
_____
_____
_____
_____
_____
_____
_____
_____
_____
_____
_____
_____
_____
_____
_____
_____
_____

A Walk To Remember

Date: _____

Location: _____

Weather: _____

Company:

_____
_____
_____

Key Memorable Moments:

_____
_____
_____
_____
_____
_____
_____

Write About The Walk:

_____
_____
_____
_____
_____
_____
_____
_____
_____
_____
_____
_____
_____
_____
_____
_____
_____
_____
_____
_____
_____
_____
_____
_____
_____
_____
_____
_____
_____

Rate Your Walk:

Spectacular   Terrible

1   2   3   4   5

Would You Go On This Walk Again & Why?:

_____
_____
_____
_____
_____
_____
_____
_____
_____
_____
_____
_____
_____
_____
_____
_____

A Walk To Remember

Date: _____

Location: _____

Weather: _____

Company:

_____
_____
_____

Key Memorable Moments:

_____
_____
_____
_____
_____
_____
_____

Write About The Walk:

_____
_____
_____
_____
_____
_____
_____
_____
_____
_____
_____
_____
_____
_____
_____
_____
_____
_____
_____
_____
_____
_____
_____
_____
_____
_____
_____
_____
_____
_____
_____

Rate Your Walk:

Spectacular   Terrible

1   2   3   4   5

Would You Go On This Walk Again & Why?:

_____
_____
_____
_____
_____
_____
_____
_____
_____
_____
_____
_____
_____
_____
_____
_____

A Walk To Remember

Date: _____

Location: _____

Weather: _____

Company:

_____
_____
_____

Key Memorable Moments:

_____
_____
_____
_____
_____
_____
_____

Write About The Walk:

_____
_____
_____
_____
_____
_____
_____
_____
_____
_____
_____
_____
_____
_____
_____
_____
_____
_____
_____
_____
_____
_____
_____
_____
_____
_____
_____
_____
_____
_____

Rate Your Walk:

Spectacular   Terrible

1   2   3   4   5

Would You Go On This Walk Again & Why?:

_____
_____
_____
_____
_____
_____
_____
_____
_____
_____
_____
_____
_____
_____
_____
_____
_____

A Walk To Remember

Date: _____

Location: _____

Weather: _____

Company:

_____
_____
_____

Key Memorable Moments:

_____
_____
_____
_____
_____
_____
_____

Write About The Walk:

_____
_____
_____
_____
_____
_____
_____
_____
_____
_____
_____
_____
_____
_____
_____
_____
_____
_____
_____
_____
_____
_____
_____
_____
_____
_____
_____
_____

Rate Your Walk:

<u>Spectacular</u>   <u>Terrible</u>

1   2   3   4   5

Would You Go On This Walk Again & Why?:

_____
_____
_____
_____
_____
_____
_____
_____
_____
_____
_____
_____
_____
_____
_____

A Walk To Remember

Date: _____

Location: _____

Weather: _____

Company:

_____
_____
_____

Key Memorable Moments:

_____
_____
_____
_____
_____
_____
_____

Write About The Walk:

_____

_____

_____

_____

_____

_____

_____

_____

_____

_____

_____

_____

_____

_____

_____

_____

_____

_____

_____

_____

_____

_____

_____

_____

_____

_____

_____

_____

_____

_____

Rate Your Walk:

<u>Spectacular</u>   <u>Terrible</u>

1   2   3   4   5

Would You Go On This Walk Again & Why?:

_____
_____
_____
_____
_____
_____
_____
_____
_____
_____
_____
_____
_____
_____
_____
_____

A Walk To Remember

Date: _____

Location: _____

Weather: _____

Company:

_____
_____
_____

Key Memorable Moments:

_____
_____
_____
_____
_____
_____
_____

Write About The Walk:

_____
_____
_____
_____
_____
_____
_____
_____
_____
_____
_____
_____
_____
_____
_____
_____
_____
_____
_____
_____
_____
_____
_____
_____
_____
_____
_____
_____
_____

Rate Your Walk:

<u>Spectacular</u>   <u>Terrible</u>

1   2   3   4   5

Would You Go On This Walk Again & Why?:

_____
_____
_____
_____
_____
_____
_____
_____
_____
_____
_____
_____
_____
_____
_____
_____
_____

A Walk To Remember

Date: _____

Location: _____

Weather: _____

Company:

_____
_____
_____

Key Memorable Moments:

_____
_____
_____
_____
_____
_____
_____
_____

Write About The Walk:

_____

_____

_____

_____

_____

_____

_____

_____

_____

_____

_____

_____

_____

_____

_____

_____

_____

_____

_____

_____

_____

_____

_____

_____

_____

_____

_____

_____

_____

_____

Rate Your Walk:

<u>Spectacular</u>   <u>Terrible</u>

1   2   3   4   5

Would You Go On This Walk Again & Why?:

_____
_____
_____
_____
_____
_____
_____
_____
_____
_____
_____
_____
_____
_____
_____
_____

A Walk To Remember

Date: _____

Location: _____

Weather: _____

Company:

_____
_____
_____

Key Memorable Moments:

_____
_____
_____
_____
_____
_____
_____

Write About The Walk:

_____
_____
_____
_____
_____
_____
_____
_____
_____
_____
_____
_____
_____
_____
_____
_____
_____
_____
_____
_____
_____
_____
_____
_____
_____
_____
_____
_____
_____
_____
_____
_____
_____
_____

Rate Your Walk:

<u>Spectacular</u>   <u>Terrible</u>

1   2   3   4   5

Would You Go On This Walk Again & Why?:

_____
_____
_____
_____
_____
_____
_____
_____
_____
_____
_____
_____
_____
_____
_____
_____

A Walk To Remember

Date: _____

Location: _____

Weather: _____

Company:

_____
_____
_____

Key Memorable Moments:

_____
_____
_____
_____
_____
_____
_____

Write About The Walk:

_____

_____

_____

_____

_____

_____

_____

_____

_____

_____

_____

_____

_____

_____

_____

_____

_____

_____

_____

_____

_____

_____

_____

_____

_____

_____

_____

_____

_____

_____

_____

_____

Rate Your Walk:

Spectacular   Terrible

1   2   3   4   5

Would You Go On This Walk Again & Why?:

_____
_____
_____
_____
_____
_____
_____
_____
_____
_____
_____
_____
_____
_____
_____
_____

A Walk To Remember

Date: _____

Location: _____

Weather: _____

Company:

_____
_____
_____

Key Memorable Moments:

_____
_____
_____
_____
_____
_____
_____

Write About The Walk:

_____
_____
_____
_____
_____
_____
_____
_____
_____
_____
_____
_____
_____
_____
_____
_____
_____
_____
_____
_____
_____
_____
_____
_____
_____
_____
_____
_____
_____
_____
_____

Rate Your Walk:

Spectacular   Terrible

1   2   3   4   5

Would You Go On This Walk Again & Why?:

_____
_____
_____
_____
_____
_____
_____
_____
_____
_____
_____
_____
_____
_____
_____
_____
_____

A Walk To Remember

Date: _____

Location: _____

Weather: _____

Company:

_____

_____

_____

Key Memorable Moments:

_____

_____

_____

_____

_____

_____

_____

_____

Write About The Walk:

Rate Your Walk:

<u>Spectacular</u>   <u>Terrible</u>

1   2   3   4   5

Would You Go On This Walk Again & Why?:

_____
_____
_____
_____
_____
_____
_____
_____
_____
_____
_____
_____
_____
_____
_____
_____

A Walk To Remember

Date: _____

Location: _____

Weather: _____

Company:

_____
_____
_____

Key Memorable Moments:

_____
_____
_____
_____
_____
_____
_____

Write About The Walk:

_____
_____
_____
_____
_____
_____
_____
_____
_____
_____
_____
_____
_____
_____
_____
_____
_____
_____
_____
_____
_____
_____
_____
_____
_____
_____

Rate Your Walk:

<u>Spectacular</u>   <u>Terrible</u>

1   2   3   4   5

Would You Go On This Walk Again & Why?:

_____
_____
_____
_____
_____
_____
_____
_____
_____
_____
_____
_____
_____
_____
_____

A Walk To Remember

Date: _____

Location: _____

Weather: _____

Company:

_____
_____
_____

Key Memorable Moments:

_____
_____
_____
_____
_____
_____
_____

Write About The Walk:

_____

_____

_____

_____

_____

_____

_____

_____

_____

_____

_____

_____

_____

_____

_____

_____

_____

_____

_____

_____

_____

_____

_____

_____

_____

_____

_____

_____

_____

_____

Rate Your Walk:

<u>Spectacular</u>　　　　　　　　　　　　　　　　　　<u>Terrible</u>

1　　　　　　2　　　　　　3　　　　　　4　　　　　　5

Would You Go On This Walk Again & Why?:

_____
_____
_____
_____
_____
_____
_____
_____
_____
_____
_____
_____
_____
_____
_____
_____
_____
_____

A Walk To Remember

Date: _____

Location: _____

Weather: _____

Company:

_____
_____
_____

Key Memorable Moments:

_____
_____
_____
_____
_____
_____
_____

Write About The Walk:

_____
_____
_____
_____
_____
_____
_____
_____
_____
_____
_____
_____
_____
_____
_____
_____
_____
_____
_____
_____
_____
_____
_____
_____
_____
_____
_____
_____

Rate Your Walk:

<u>Spectacular</u>   <u>Terrible</u>

1   2   3   4   5

Would You Go On This Walk Again & Why?:

_____
_____
_____
_____
_____
_____
_____
_____
_____
_____
_____
_____
_____
_____
_____
_____

A Walk To Remember

Date: _____

Location: _____

Weather: _____

Company:

_____
_____
_____

Key Memorable Moments:

_____
_____
_____
_____
_____
_____
_____

Write About The Walk:

_____

_____

_____

_____

_____

_____

_____

_____

_____

_____

_____

_____

_____

_____

_____

_____

_____

_____

_____

_____

_____

_____

_____

_____

_____

_____

_____

_____

_____

_____

_____

_____

Rate Your Walk:

<u>Spectacular</u>   <u>Terrible</u>

1   2   3   4   5

Would You Go On This Walk Again & Why?:

_____
_____
_____
_____
_____
_____
_____
_____
_____
_____
_____
_____
_____
_____
_____

A Walk To Remember

Date: _____

Location: _____

Weather: _____

Company:

_____
_____
_____

Key Memorable Moments:

_____
_____
_____
_____
_____
_____
_____

Write About The Walk:

_____
_____
_____
_____
_____
_____
_____
_____
_____
_____
_____
_____
_____
_____
_____
_____
_____
_____
_____
_____
_____
_____
_____
_____
_____
_____
_____
_____
_____

Rate Your Walk:

Spectacular   Terrible

1   2   3   4   5

Would You Go On This Walk Again & Why?:

_____
_____
_____
_____
_____
_____
_____
_____
_____
_____
_____
_____
_____
_____
_____
_____

A Walk To Remember

Date: _____

Location: _____

Weather: _____

Company:

_____
_____
_____

Key Memorable Moments:

_____
_____
_____
_____
_____
_____
_____

Write About The Walk:

_____
_____
_____
_____
_____
_____
_____
_____
_____
_____
_____
_____
_____
_____
_____
_____
_____
_____
_____
_____
_____
_____
_____
_____
_____
_____

Rate Your Walk:

<u>Spectacular</u>   <u>Terrible</u>

1   2   3   4   5

Would You Go On This Walk Again & Why?:

_____
_____
_____
_____
_____
_____
_____
_____
_____
_____
_____
_____
_____
_____
_____
_____

A Walk To Remember

Date: _____

Location: _____

Weather: _____

Company:

_____
_____
_____

Key Memorable Moments:

_____
_____
_____
_____
_____
_____
_____

Write About The Walk:

_____
_____
_____
_____
_____
_____
_____
_____
_____
_____
_____
_____
_____
_____
_____
_____
_____
_____
_____
_____
_____
_____
_____
_____
_____
_____
_____
_____
_____
_____
_____
_____
_____

Rate Your Walk:

<u>Spectacular</u>   <u>Terrible</u>

1   2   3   4   5

Would You Go On This Walk Again & Why?:

_____
_____
_____
_____
_____
_____
_____
_____
_____
_____
_____
_____
_____
_____
_____
_____

A Walk To Remember

Date: _____

Location: _____

Weather: _____

Company:

_____
_____
_____

Key Memorable Moments:

_____
_____
_____
_____
_____
_____
_____

Write About The Walk:

_____

_____

_____

_____

_____

_____

_____

_____

_____

_____

_____

_____

_____

_____

_____

_____

_____

_____

_____

_____

_____

_____

_____

_____

_____

_____

_____

_____

_____

_____

_____

Rate Your Walk:

<u>Spectacular</u>   <u>Terrible</u>

1   2   3   4   5

Would You Go On This Walk Again & Why?:

_____
_____
_____
_____
_____
_____
_____
_____
_____
_____
_____
_____
_____
_____
_____
_____

A Walk To Remember

Date: _____

Location: _____

Weather: _____

Company:

_____
_____
_____

Key Memorable Moments:

_____
_____
_____
_____
_____
_____
_____

Write About The Walk:

_____

_____

_____

_____

_____

_____

_____

_____

_____

_____

_____

_____

_____

_____

_____

_____

_____

_____

_____

_____

_____

_____

_____

_____

_____

_____

_____

_____

_____

_____

Rate Your Walk:

<u>Spectacular</u>   <u>Terrible</u>

1   2   3   4   5

Would You Go On This Walk Again & Why?:

_____
_____
_____
_____
_____
_____
_____
_____
_____
_____
_____
_____
_____
_____
_____
_____
_____

<u>A Walk To Remember</u>

Date: _____

Location: _____

Weather: _____

Company:

_____
_____
_____

Key Memorable Moments:

_____
_____
_____
_____
_____
_____
_____

Write About The Walk:

_____

_____

_____

_____

_____

_____

_____

_____

_____

_____

_____

_____

_____

_____

_____

_____

_____

_____

_____

_____

_____

_____

_____

_____

_____

_____

_____

_____

_____

_____

_____

_____

_____

Rate Your Walk:

Spectacular   Terrible

1   2   3   4   5

Would You Go On This Walk Again & Why?:

_____
_____
_____
_____
_____
_____
_____
_____
_____
_____
_____
_____
_____
_____
_____

A Walk To Remember

Date: _____

Location: _____

Weather: _____

Company:

_____

_____

_____

Key Memorable Moments:

_____

_____

_____

_____

_____

_____

_____

Write About The Walk:

_____
_____
_____
_____
_____
_____
_____
_____
_____
_____
_____
_____
_____
_____
_____
_____
_____
_____
_____
_____
_____
_____
_____
_____
_____
_____
_____
_____
_____
_____

Rate Your Walk:

<u>Spectacular</u>   <u>Terrible</u>

1   2   3   4   5

Would You Go On This Walk Again & Why?:

_____
_____
_____
_____
_____
_____
_____
_____
_____
_____
_____
_____
_____
_____
_____
_____

A Walk To Remember

Date: _____

Location: _____

Weather: _____

Company:

_____
_____
_____

Key Memorable Moments:

_____
_____
_____
_____
_____
_____
_____

Write About The Walk:

_____
_____
_____
_____
_____
_____
_____
_____
_____
_____
_____
_____
_____
_____
_____
_____
_____
_____
_____
_____
_____
_____
_____
_____
_____
_____
_____
_____
_____
_____

Rate Your Walk:

Spectacular   Terrible

1   2   3   4   5

Would You Go On This Walk Again & Why?:

_____
_____
_____
_____
_____
_____
_____
_____
_____
_____
_____
_____
_____
_____
_____
_____

A Walk To Remember

Date: _____

Location: _____

Weather: _____

Company:

_____
_____
_____

Key Memorable Moments:

_____
_____
_____
_____
_____
_____
_____

Write About The Walk:

_____
_____
_____
_____
_____
_____
_____
_____
_____
_____
_____
_____
_____
_____
_____
_____
_____
_____
_____
_____
_____
_____
_____
_____
_____
_____
_____
_____
_____
_____
_____
_____

Rate Your Walk:

<u>Spectacular</u>   <u>Terrible</u>

1   2   3   4   5

Would You Go On This Walk Again & Why?:

_____
_____
_____
_____
_____
_____
_____
_____
_____
_____
_____
_____
_____
_____
_____
_____
_____

A Walk To Remember

Date: _____

Location: _____

Weather: _____

Company:

_____

_____

_____

Key Memorable Moments:

_____

_____

_____

_____

_____

_____

_____

Write About The Walk:

_____
_____
_____
_____
_____
_____
_____
_____
_____
_____
_____
_____
_____
_____
_____
_____
_____
_____
_____
_____
_____
_____
_____
_____
_____
_____
_____
_____
_____
_____
_____

Rate Your Walk:

Spectacular   Terrible

1   2   3   4   5

Would You Go On This Walk Again & Why?:

_____
_____
_____
_____
_____
_____
_____
_____
_____
_____
_____
_____
_____
_____
_____
_____
_____

A Walk To Remember

Date: _____

Location: _____

Weather: _____

Company:

_____
_____
_____

Key Memorable Moments:

_____
_____
_____
_____
_____
_____
_____

Write About The Walk:

_____
_____
_____
_____
_____
_____
_____
_____
_____
_____
_____
_____
_____
_____
_____
_____
_____
_____
_____
_____
_____
_____
_____
_____
_____
_____
_____
_____
_____

Rate Your Walk:

Spectacular   Terrible

1   2   3   4   5

Would You Go On This Walk Again & Why?:

_____
_____
_____
_____
_____
_____
_____
_____
_____
_____
_____
_____
_____
_____
_____
_____
_____

A Walk To Remember

Date: _____

Location: _____

Weather: _____

Company:

_____
_____
_____

Key Memorable Moments:

_____
_____
_____
_____
_____
_____
_____

Write About The Walk:

_____

_____

_____

_____

_____

_____

_____

_____

_____

_____

_____

_____

_____

_____

_____

_____

_____

_____

_____

_____

_____

_____

_____

_____

_____

_____

_____

_____

_____

Rate Your Walk:

Spectacular   Terrible

1   2   3   4   5

Would You Go On This Walk Again & Why?:

_____
_____
_____
_____
_____
_____
_____
_____
_____
_____
_____
_____
_____
_____
_____
_____
_____

A Walk To Remember

Date: _____

Location: _____

Weather: _____

Company:

_____
_____
_____

Key Memorable Moments:

_____
_____
_____
_____
_____
_____
_____

Write About The Walk:

_____

_____

_____

_____

_____

_____

_____

_____

_____

_____

_____

_____

_____

_____

_____

_____

_____

_____

_____

_____

_____

_____

_____

_____

_____

_____

_____

_____

_____

_____

_____

_____

_____

_____

Rate Your Walk:

<u>Spectacular</u>   <u>Terrible</u>

1   2   3   4   5

Would You Go On This Walk Again & Why?:

_____
_____
_____
_____
_____
_____
_____
_____
_____
_____
_____
_____
_____
_____
_____
_____
_____

A Walk To Remember

Date: _____

Location: _____

Weather: _____

Company:

_____
_____
_____

Key Memorable Moments:

_____
_____
_____
_____
_____
_____
_____

Write About The Walk:

_____
_____
_____
_____
_____
_____
_____
_____
_____
_____
_____
_____
_____
_____
_____
_____
_____
_____
_____
_____
_____
_____
_____
_____
_____
_____
_____
_____
_____
_____

Rate Your Walk:

Spectacular   Terrible

1   2   3   4   5

Would You Go On This Walk Again & Why?:

_____
_____
_____
_____
_____
_____
_____
_____
_____
_____
_____
_____
_____
_____
_____
_____

A Walk To Remember

Date: _____

Location: _____

Weather: _____

Company:

_____
_____
_____

Key Memorable Moments:

_____
_____
_____
_____
_____
_____
_____

Write About The Walk:

_____

_____

_____

_____

_____

_____

_____

_____

_____

_____

_____

_____

_____

_____

_____

_____

_____

_____

_____

_____

_____

_____

_____

_____

_____

_____

_____

_____

_____

_____

_____

_____

Rate Your Walk:

<u>Spectacular</u>   <u>Terrible</u>

1   2   3   4   5

Would You Go On This Walk Again & Why?:

_____
_____
_____
_____
_____
_____
_____
_____
_____
_____
_____
_____
_____
_____
_____
_____
_____

A Walk To Remember

Date: _____

Location: _____

Weather: _____

Company:

_____

_____

_____

Key Memorable Moments:

_____

_____

_____

_____

_____

_____

_____

Write About The Walk:

_____

_____

_____

_____

_____

_____

_____

_____

_____

_____

_____

_____

_____

_____

_____

_____

_____

_____

_____

_____

_____

_____

_____

_____

_____

_____

_____

_____

_____

_____

_____

_____

_____

Rate Your Walk:

<u>Spectacular</u>　　　　　　　　　　　　　　　　　<u>Terrible</u>

1　　　　　　2　　　　　　3　　　　　　4　　　　　　5

Would You Go On This Walk Again & Why?:

_____
_____
_____
_____
_____
_____
_____
_____
_____
_____
_____
_____
_____
_____
_____
_____

A Walk To Remember

Date: _____

Location: _____

Weather: _____

Company:

_____
_____
_____

Key Memorable Moments:

_____
_____
_____
_____
_____
_____
_____
_____

Write About The Walk:

_____

_____

_____

_____

_____

_____

_____

_____

_____

_____

_____

_____

_____

_____

_____

_____

_____

_____

_____

_____

_____

_____

_____

_____

_____

_____

_____

_____

_____

_____

Rate Your Walk:

<u>Spectacular</u>   <u>Terrible</u>

1   2   3   4   5

Would You Go On This Walk Again & Why?:

_____
_____
_____
_____
_____
_____
_____
_____
_____
_____
_____
_____
_____
_____
_____
_____
_____
_____

A Walk To Remember

Date: _____

Location: _____

Weather: _____

Company:

_____
_____
_____

Key Memorable Moments:

_____
_____
_____
_____
_____
_____
_____

Write About The Walk:

_____
_____
_____
_____
_____
_____
_____
_____
_____
_____
_____
_____
_____
_____
_____
_____
_____
_____
_____
_____
_____
_____
_____
_____
_____
_____
_____
_____
_____
_____

Rate Your Walk:

Spectacular   Terrible

1   2   3   4   5

Would You Go On This Walk Again & Why?:

_____
_____
_____
_____
_____
_____
_____
_____
_____
_____
_____
_____
_____
_____
_____
_____

<u>A Walk To Remember</u>

Date: _____

Location: _____

Weather: _____

Company:

_____
_____
_____

Key Memorable Moments:

_____
_____
_____
_____
_____
_____
_____

Write About The Walk:

_____
_____
_____
_____
_____
_____
_____
_____
_____
_____
_____
_____
_____
_____
_____
_____
_____
_____
_____
_____
_____
_____
_____
_____
_____
_____
_____
_____
_____
_____
_____

Rate Your Walk:

<u>Spectacular</u>   <u>Terrible</u>

1   2   3   4   5

Would You Go On This Walk Again & Why?:

_____
_____
_____
_____
_____
_____
_____
_____
_____
_____
_____
_____
_____
_____
_____
_____

A Walk To Remember

Date: _____

Location: _____

Weather: _____

Company:

_____
_____
_____

Key Memorable Moments:

_____
_____
_____
_____
_____
_____
_____

Write About The Walk:

_____

_____

_____

_____

_____

_____

_____

_____

_____

_____

_____

_____

_____

_____

_____

_____

_____

_____

_____

_____

_____

_____

_____

_____

_____

_____

_____

_____

_____

_____

_____

Rate Your Walk:

Spectacular   Terrible

1   2   3   4   5

Would You Go On This Walk Again & Why?:

_____
_____
_____
_____
_____
_____
_____
_____
_____
_____
_____
_____
_____
_____
_____
_____

A Walk To Remember

Date: _____

Location: _____

Weather: _____

Company:

_____
_____
_____

Key Memorable Moments:

_____
_____
_____
_____
_____
_____
_____

Write About The Walk:

_____
_____
_____
_____
_____
_____
_____
_____
_____
_____
_____
_____
_____
_____
_____
_____
_____
_____
_____
_____
_____
_____
_____
_____
_____
_____
_____
_____
_____
_____

Rate Your Walk:

Spectacular   Terrible

1   2   3   4   5

Would You Go On This Walk Again & Why?:

_____
_____
_____
_____
_____
_____
_____
_____
_____
_____
_____
_____
_____
_____
_____
_____
_____
_____
_____

A Walk To Remember

Date: _____

Location: _____

Weather: _____

Company:

_____
_____
_____

Key Memorable Moments:

_____
_____
_____
_____
_____
_____
_____

Write About The Walk:

_____
_____
_____
_____
_____
_____
_____
_____
_____
_____
_____
_____
_____
_____
_____
_____
_____
_____
_____
_____
_____
_____
_____
_____
_____
_____
_____
_____
_____
_____
_____
_____

Rate Your Walk:

<u>Spectacular</u>   <u>Terrible</u>

1   2   3   4   5

Would You Go On This Walk Again & Why?:

_____
_____
_____
_____
_____
_____
_____
_____
_____
_____
_____
_____
_____
_____
_____
_____
_____

A Walk To Remember

Date: _____

Location: _____

Weather: _____

Company:

_____
_____
_____

Key Memorable Moments:

_____
_____
_____
_____
_____
_____
_____

Write About The Walk:

_____
_____
_____
_____
_____
_____
_____
_____
_____
_____
_____
_____
_____
_____
_____
_____
_____
_____
_____
_____
_____
_____
_____
_____
_____
_____
_____
_____
_____

Rate Your Walk:

Spectacular   Terrible

1   2   3   4   5

Would You Go On This Walk Again & Why?:

_____
_____
_____
_____
_____
_____
_____
_____
_____
_____
_____
_____
_____
_____
_____
_____
_____
_____

A Walk To Remember

Date: _____

Location: _____

Weather: _____

Company:

_____

_____

_____

Key Memorable Moments:

_____

_____

_____

_____

_____

_____

_____

Write About The Walk:

_____

_____

_____

_____

_____

_____

_____

_____

_____

_____

_____

_____

_____

_____

_____

_____

_____

_____

_____

_____

_____

_____

_____

_____

_____

_____

_____

_____

_____

Rate Your Walk:

Spectacular   Terrible

1   2   3   4   5

Would You Go On This Walk Again & Why?:

_____
_____
_____
_____
_____
_____
_____
_____
_____
_____
_____
_____
_____
_____
_____
_____

A Walk To Remember

Date: _____

Location: _____

Weather: _____

Company:

_____
_____
_____

Key Memorable Moments:

_____
_____
_____
_____
_____
_____
_____

Write About The Walk:

_____
_____
_____
_____
_____
_____
_____
_____
_____
_____
_____
_____
_____
_____
_____
_____
_____
_____
_____
_____
_____
_____
_____
_____
_____
_____
_____
_____
_____
_____
_____

Rate Your Walk:

<u>Spectacular</u>   <u>Terrible</u>

1   2   3   4   5

Would You Go On This Walk Again & Why?:

_____
_____
_____
_____
_____
_____
_____
_____
_____
_____
_____
_____
_____
_____
_____

A Walk To Remember

Date: _____

Location: _____

Weather: _____

Company:

_____
_____
_____

Key Memorable Moments:

_____
_____
_____
_____
_____
_____
_____

Write About The Walk:

_____
_____
_____
_____
_____
_____
_____
_____
_____
_____
_____
_____
_____
_____
_____
_____
_____
_____
_____
_____
_____
_____
_____
_____
_____
_____
_____

Rate Your Walk:

Spectacular   Terrible

1   2   3   4   5

Would You Go On This Walk Again & Why?:

_____
_____
_____
_____
_____
_____
_____
_____
_____
_____
_____
_____
_____
_____
_____

A Walk To Remember

Date: _____

Location: _____

Weather: _____

Company:

_____
_____
_____

Key Memorable Moments:

_____
_____
_____
_____
_____
_____
_____
_____

Write About The Walk:

_____
_____
_____
_____
_____
_____
_____
_____
_____
_____
_____
_____
_____
_____
_____
_____
_____
_____
_____
_____
_____
_____
_____
_____
_____
_____
_____
_____
_____
_____
_____
_____
_____

Rate Your Walk:

<u>Spectacular</u>   <u>Terrible</u>

1   2   3   4   5

Would You Go On This Walk Again & Why?:

_____
_____
_____
_____
_____
_____
_____
_____
_____
_____
_____
_____
_____
_____
_____
_____

A Walk To Remember

Date: _____

Location: _____

Weather: _____

Company:

_____
_____
_____

Key Memorable Moments:

_____
_____
_____
_____
_____
_____
_____

Write About The Walk:

_____
_____
_____
_____
_____
_____
_____
_____
_____
_____
_____
_____
_____
_____
_____
_____
_____
_____
_____
_____
_____
_____
_____
_____
_____
_____
_____
_____
_____
_____
_____

Rate Your Walk:

<u>Spectacular</u>   <u>Terrible</u>

1   2   3   4   5

Would You Go On This Walk Again & Why?:

_____
_____
_____
_____
_____
_____
_____
_____
_____
_____
_____
_____
_____
_____
_____
_____

A Walk To Remember

Date: _____

Location: _____

Weather: _____

Company:

_____
_____
_____

Key Memorable Moments:

_____
_____
_____
_____
_____
_____
_____

Write About The Walk:

_____
_____
_____
_____
_____
_____
_____
_____
_____
_____
_____
_____
_____
_____
_____
_____
_____
_____
_____
_____
_____
_____
_____
_____
_____
_____
_____
_____

Rate Your Walk:

Spectacular   Terrible

1   2   3   4   5

Would You Go On This Walk Again & Why?:

_____
_____
_____
_____
_____
_____
_____
_____
_____
_____
_____
_____
_____
_____
_____
_____

A Walk To Remember

Date: _____

Location: _____

Weather: _____

Company:

_____
_____
_____

Key Memorable Moments:

_____
_____
_____
_____
_____
_____
_____

Write About The Walk:

_____
_____
_____
_____
_____
_____
_____
_____
_____
_____
_____
_____
_____
_____
_____
_____
_____
_____
_____
_____
_____
_____
_____
_____
_____
_____
_____
_____
_____
_____
_____
_____

Rate Your Walk:

Spectacular   Terrible

1   2   3   4   5

Would You Go On This Walk Again & Why?:

_____
_____
_____
_____
_____
_____
_____
_____
_____
_____
_____
_____
_____
_____
_____
_____

A Walk To Remember

Date: _____

Location: _____

Weather: _____

Company:

_____
_____
_____

Key Memorable Moments:

_____
_____
_____
_____
_____
_____
_____

Write About The Walk:

_____
_____
_____
_____
_____
_____
_____
_____
_____
_____
_____
_____
_____
_____
_____
_____
_____
_____
_____
_____
_____
_____
_____
_____
_____
_____
_____
_____
_____

Rate Your Walk:

<u>Spectacular</u>　　　　　　　　　　　　　　　　<u>Terrible</u>

1　　　　　　2　　　　　　3　　　　　　4　　　　　　5

Would You Go On This Walk Again & Why?:

_____
_____
_____
_____
_____
_____
_____
_____
_____
_____
_____
_____
_____
_____
_____
_____
_____

A Walk To Remember

Date: _____

Location: _____

Weather: _____

Company:

_____
_____
_____

Key Memorable Moments:

_____
_____
_____
_____
_____
_____
_____

Write About The Walk:

_____

_____

_____

_____

_____

_____

_____

_____

_____

_____

_____

_____

_____

_____

_____

_____

_____

_____

_____

_____

_____

_____

_____

_____

_____

_____

_____

_____

_____

Rate Your Walk:

<u>Spectacular</u>   <u>Terrible</u>

1   2   3   4   5

Would You Go On This Walk Again & Why?:

_____
_____
_____
_____
_____
_____
_____
_____
_____
_____
_____
_____
_____
_____
_____
_____
_____

A Walk To Remember

Date: _____

Location: _____

Weather: _____

Company:

_____
_____
_____

Key Memorable Moments:

_____
_____
_____
_____
_____
_____
_____

Write About The Walk:

_____

_____

_____

_____

_____

_____

_____

_____

_____

_____

_____

_____

_____

_____

_____

_____

_____

_____

_____

_____

_____

_____

_____

_____

_____

_____

_____

_____

_____

_____

_____

_____

Rate Your Walk:

<u>Spectacular</u>   <u>Terrible</u>

1   2   3   4   5

Would You Go On This Walk Again & Why?:

_____
_____
_____
_____
_____
_____
_____
_____
_____
_____
_____
_____
_____
_____
_____
_____

A Walk To Remember

Date: _____

Location: _____

Weather: _____

Company:

_____
_____
_____

Key Memorable Moments:

_____
_____
_____
_____
_____
_____
_____

Write About The Walk:

_____

_____

_____

_____

_____

_____

_____

_____

_____

_____

_____

_____

_____

_____

_____

_____

_____

_____

_____

_____

_____

_____

_____

_____

_____

_____

_____

_____

_____

_____

_____

_____

Rate Your Walk:

Spectacular   Terrible

1   2   3   4   5

Would You Go On This Walk Again & Why?:

_____
_____
_____
_____
_____
_____
_____
_____
_____
_____
_____
_____
_____
_____
_____
_____
_____

A Walk To Remember

Date: _____

Location: _____

Weather: _____

Company:

_____
_____
_____

Key Memorable Moments:

_____
_____
_____
_____
_____
_____
_____

Write About The Walk:

_____
_____
_____
_____
_____
_____
_____
_____
_____
_____
_____
_____
_____
_____
_____
_____
_____
_____
_____
_____
_____
_____
_____
_____
_____
_____
_____
_____
_____
_____

Rate Your Walk:

<u>Spectacular</u>   <u>Terrible</u>

1   2   3   4   5

Would You Go On This Walk Again & Why?:

_____
_____
_____
_____
_____
_____
_____
_____
_____
_____
_____
_____
_____
_____
_____
_____
_____
_____

A Walk To Remember

Date: _____

Location: _____

Weather: _____

Company:

_____
_____
_____

Key Memorable Moments:

_____
_____
_____
_____
_____
_____
_____

Write About The Walk:

_____
_____
_____
_____
_____
_____
_____
_____
_____
_____
_____
_____
_____
_____
_____
_____
_____
_____
_____
_____
_____
_____
_____
_____
_____
_____
_____
_____
_____
_____
_____

Rate Your Walk:

<u>Spectacular</u>   <u>Terrible</u>

1   2   3   4   5

Would You Go On This Walk Again & Why?:

_____
_____
_____
_____
_____
_____
_____
_____
_____
_____
_____
_____
_____
_____
_____
_____
_____

A Walk To Remember

Date: _____

Location: _____

Weather: _____

Company:

_____
_____
_____

Key Memorable Moments:

_____
_____
_____
_____
_____
_____
_____

Write About The Walk:

_____
_____
_____
_____
_____
_____
_____
_____
_____
_____
_____
_____
_____
_____
_____
_____
_____
_____
_____
_____
_____
_____
_____
_____
_____
_____
_____
_____
_____
_____
_____
_____

Rate Your Walk:

<u>Spectacular</u>   <u>Terrible</u>

1   2   3   4   5

Would You Go On This Walk Again & Why?:

_____
_____
_____
_____
_____
_____
_____
_____
_____
_____
_____
_____
_____
_____
_____
_____
_____

A Walk To Remember

Date: _____

Location: _____

Weather: _____

Company:

_____
_____
_____

Key Memorable Moments:

_____
_____
_____
_____
_____
_____
_____

Write About The Walk:

_____
_____
_____
_____
_____
_____
_____
_____
_____
_____
_____
_____
_____
_____
_____
_____
_____
_____
_____
_____
_____
_____
_____
_____
_____
_____
_____
_____
_____

Rate Your Walk:

Spectacular　　　　　　　　　　　　　　　　　Terrible

1　　　　　2　　　　　3　　　　　4　　　　　5

Would You Go On This Walk Again & Why?:

_____
_____
_____
_____
_____
_____
_____
_____
_____
_____
_____
_____
_____
_____
_____
_____

A Walk To Remember

Date: _____

Location: _____

Weather: _____

Company:

_____
_____
_____

Key Memorable Moments:

_____
_____
_____
_____
_____
_____
_____

Write About The Walk:

_____
_____
_____
_____
_____
_____
_____
_____
_____
_____
_____
_____
_____
_____
_____
_____
_____
_____
_____
_____
_____
_____
_____
_____
_____
_____
_____
_____
_____
_____
_____
_____

Rate Your Walk:

Spectacular   Terrible

1   2   3   4   5

Would You Go On This Walk Again & Why?:

_____
_____
_____
_____
_____
_____
_____
_____
_____
_____
_____
_____
_____
_____
_____
_____
_____
_____

A Walk To Remember

Date: _____

Location: _____

Weather: _____

Company:

_____
_____
_____

Key Memorable Moments:

_____
_____
_____
_____
_____
_____
_____

Write About The Walk:

_____

_____

_____

_____

_____

_____

_____

_____

_____

_____

_____

_____

_____

_____

_____

_____

_____

_____

_____

_____

_____

_____

_____

_____

_____

_____

_____

_____

_____

Rate Your Walk:

Spectacular   Terrible

1   2   3   4   5

Would You Go On This Walk Again & Why?:

_____
_____
_____
_____
_____
_____
_____
_____
_____
_____
_____
_____
_____
_____
_____
_____

A Walk To Remember

Date: _____

Location: _____

Weather: _____

Company:

_____
_____
_____

Key Memorable Moments:

_____
_____
_____
_____
_____
_____
_____

Write About The Walk:

_____
_____
_____
_____
_____
_____
_____
_____
_____
_____
_____
_____
_____
_____
_____
_____
_____
_____
_____
_____
_____
_____
_____
_____
_____
_____
_____

Rate Your Walk:

Spectacular   Terrible

1   2   3   4   5

Would You Go On This Walk Again & Why?:

_____
_____
_____
_____
_____
_____
_____
_____
_____
_____
_____
_____
_____
_____
_____
_____
_____

A Walk To Remember

Date: _____

Location: _____

Weather: _____

Company:

_____
_____
_____

Key Memorable Moments:

_____
_____
_____
_____
_____
_____
_____

Write About The Walk:

_____
_____
_____
_____
_____
_____
_____
_____
_____
_____
_____
_____
_____
_____
_____
_____
_____
_____
_____
_____
_____
_____
_____
_____
_____
_____
_____
_____
_____
_____

Rate Your Walk:

Spectacular   Terrible

1   2   3   4   5

Would You Go On This Walk Again & Why?:

_____
_____
_____
_____
_____
_____
_____
_____
_____
_____
_____
_____
_____
_____
_____
_____

A Walk To Remember

Date: _____

Location: _____

Weather: _____

Company:

_____
_____
_____

Key Memorable Moments:

_____
_____
_____
_____
_____
_____
_____

Write About The Walk:

Rate Your Walk:

Spectacular   Terrible

1   2   3   4   5

Would You Go On This Walk Again & Why?:

_____
_____
_____
_____
_____
_____
_____
_____
_____
_____
_____
_____
_____
_____
_____
_____
_____

A Walk To Remember

Date: _____

Location: _____

Weather: _____

Company:

_____
_____
_____

Key Memorable Moments:

_____
_____
_____
_____
_____
_____
_____

Write About The Walk:

_____
_____
_____
_____
_____
_____
_____
_____
_____
_____
_____
_____
_____
_____
_____
_____
_____
_____
_____
_____
_____
_____
_____
_____
_____
_____
_____
_____
_____
_____

Rate Your Walk:

Spectacular   Terrible

1   2   3   4   5

Would You Go On This Walk Again & Why?:

_____
_____
_____
_____
_____
_____
_____
_____
_____
_____
_____
_____
_____
_____
_____
_____

A Walk To Remember

Date: _____

Location: _____

Weather: _____

Company:

_____
_____
_____

Key Memorable Moments:

_____
_____
_____
_____
_____
_____
_____

Write About The Walk:

Rate Your Walk:

<u>Spectacular</u>   <u>Terrible</u>

1   2   3   4   5

Would You Go On This Walk Again & Why?:

_____
_____
_____
_____
_____
_____
_____
_____
_____
_____
_____
_____
_____
_____
_____
_____
_____
_____

A Walk To Remember

Date: _____

Location: _____

Weather: _____

Company:

_____
_____
_____

Key Memorable Moments:

_____
_____
_____
_____
_____
_____
_____

Write About The Walk:

_____
_____
_____
_____
_____
_____
_____
_____
_____
_____
_____
_____
_____
_____
_____
_____
_____
_____
_____
_____
_____
_____
_____
_____
_____
_____
_____
_____
_____
_____

Rate Your Walk:

Spectacular   Terrible

1   2   3   4   5

Would You Go On This Walk Again & Why?:

_____
_____
_____
_____
_____
_____
_____
_____
_____
_____
_____
_____
_____
_____
_____
_____

A Walk To Remember

Date: _____

Location: _____

Weather: _____

Company:

_____
_____
_____

Key Memorable Moments:

_____
_____
_____
_____
_____
_____
_____

Write About The Walk:

_____

_____

_____

_____

_____

_____

_____

_____

_____

_____

_____

_____

_____

_____

_____

_____

_____

_____

_____

_____

_____

_____

_____

_____

_____

_____

_____

_____

_____

_____

_____

_____

_____

Rate Your Walk:

Spectacular   Terrible

1   2   3   4   5

Would You Go On This Walk Again & Why?:

_____
_____
_____
_____
_____
_____
_____
_____
_____
_____
_____
_____
_____
_____
_____
_____

A Walk To Remember

Date: _____

Location: _____

Weather: _____

Company:

_____
_____
_____

Key Memorable Moments:

_____
_____
_____
_____
_____
_____
_____

Write About The Walk:

_____

_____

_____

_____

_____

_____

_____

_____

_____

_____

_____

_____

_____

_____

_____

_____

_____

_____

_____

_____

_____

_____

_____

_____

_____

_____

_____

_____

_____

Rate Your Walk:

Spectacular   Terrible

1   2   3   4   5

Would You Go On This Walk Again & Why?:

_____
_____
_____
_____
_____
_____
_____
_____
_____
_____
_____
_____
_____
_____
_____
_____

A Walk To Remember

Date: _____

Location: _____

Weather: _____

Company:

_____
_____
_____

Key Memorable Moments:

_____
_____
_____
_____
_____
_____
_____

Write About The Walk:

_____

_____

_____

_____

_____

_____

_____

_____

_____

_____

_____

_____

_____

_____

_____

_____

_____

_____

_____

_____

_____

_____

_____

_____

_____

_____

_____

_____

Rate Your Walk:

Spectacular   Terrible

1   2   3   4   5

Would You Go On This Walk Again & Why?:

_____
_____
_____
_____
_____
_____
_____
_____
_____
_____
_____
_____
_____
_____
_____
_____

A Walk To Remember

Date: _____

Location: _____

Weather: _____

Company:

_____
_____
_____

Key Memorable Moments:

_____
_____
_____
_____
_____
_____
_____

Write About The Walk:

_____

_____

_____

_____

_____

_____

_____

_____

_____

_____

_____

_____

_____

_____

_____

_____

_____

_____

_____

_____

_____

_____

_____

_____

_____

_____

_____

_____

_____

_____

_____

Rate Your Walk:

Spectacular   Terrible

1   2   3   4   5

Would You Go On This Walk Again & Why?:

_____
_____
_____
_____
_____
_____
_____
_____
_____
_____
_____
_____
_____
_____
_____
_____
_____

A Walk To Remember

Date: _____

Location: _____

Weather: _____

Company:

_____

_____

_____

Key Memorable Moments:

_____

_____

_____

_____

_____

_____

_____

Write About The Walk:

_____

_____

_____

_____

_____

_____

_____

_____

_____

_____

_____

_____

_____

_____

_____

_____

_____

_____

_____

_____

_____

_____

_____

_____

_____

_____

_____

_____

_____

_____

_____

Rate Your Walk:

Spectacular   Terrible

1   2   3   4   5

Would You Go On This Walk Again & Why?:

_____
_____
_____
_____
_____
_____
_____
_____
_____
_____
_____
_____
_____
_____
_____
_____

A Walk To Remember

Date: _____

Location: _____

Weather: _____

Company:

_____
_____
_____

Key Memorable Moments:

_____
_____
_____
_____
_____
_____
_____

Write About The Walk:

_____

_____

_____

_____

_____

_____

_____

_____

_____

_____

_____

_____

_____

_____

_____

_____

_____

_____

_____

_____

_____

_____

_____

_____

_____

_____

_____

_____

_____

_____

_____

_____

_____

_____

_____

Rate Your Walk:

Spectacular   Terrible

1   2   3   4   5

Would You Go On This Walk Again & Why?:

_____
_____
_____
_____
_____
_____
_____
_____
_____
_____
_____
_____
_____
_____
_____
_____
_____

A Walk To Remember

Date: _____

Location: _____

Weather: _____

Company:

_____
_____
_____

Key Memorable Moments:

_____
_____
_____
_____
_____
_____
_____

Write About The Walk:

_____

_____

_____

_____

_____

_____

_____

_____

_____

_____

_____

_____

_____

_____

_____

_____

_____

_____

_____

_____

_____

_____

_____

_____

_____

_____

_____

_____

_____

_____

Rate Your Walk:

<u>Spectacular</u>   <u>Terrible</u>

1   2   3   4   5

Would You Go On This Walk Again & Why?:

_____
_____
_____
_____
_____
_____
_____
_____
_____
_____
_____
_____
_____
_____
_____
_____
_____

A Walk To Remember

Date: _____

Location: _____

Weather: _____

Company:

_____
_____
_____

Key Memorable Moments:

_____
_____
_____
_____
_____
_____
_____

Write About The Walk:

_____

_____

_____

_____

_____

_____

_____

_____

_____

_____

_____

_____

_____

_____

_____

_____

_____

_____

_____

_____

_____

_____

_____

_____

_____

_____

_____

_____

_____

Rate Your Walk:

Spectacular   Terrible

1   2   3   4   5

Would You Go On This Walk Again & Why?:

_____
_____
_____
_____
_____
_____
_____
_____
_____
_____
_____
_____
_____
_____
_____
_____
_____

A Walk To Remember

Date: _____

Location: _____

Weather: _____

Company:

_____
_____
_____

Key Memorable Moments:

_____
_____
_____
_____
_____
_____
_____

Write About The Walk:

_____

_____

_____

_____

_____

_____

_____

_____

_____

_____

_____

_____

_____

_____

_____

_____

_____

_____

_____

_____

_____

_____

_____

_____

_____

_____

_____

_____

_____

_____

Rate Your Walk:

<u>Spectacular</u>   <u>Terrible</u>

1   2   3   4   5

Would You Go On This Walk Again & Why?:

_____
_____
_____
_____
_____
_____
_____
_____
_____
_____
_____
_____
_____
_____
_____
_____
_____

A Walk To Remember

Date: _____

Location: _____

Weather: _____

Company:

_____
_____
_____

Key Memorable Moments:

_____
_____
_____
_____
_____
_____
_____

Write About The Walk:

_____

_____

_____

_____

_____

_____

_____

_____

_____

_____

_____

_____

_____

_____

_____

_____

_____

_____

_____

_____

_____

_____

_____

_____

_____

_____

_____

_____

_____

_____

_____

_____

Rate Your Walk:

Spectacular   Terrible

1   2   3   4   5

Would You Go On This Walk Again & Why?:

_____
_____
_____
_____
_____
_____
_____
_____
_____
_____
_____
_____
_____
_____
_____

A Walk To Remember

Date: _____

Location: _____

Weather: _____

Company:

_____
_____
_____

Key Memorable Moments:

_____
_____
_____
_____
_____
_____
_____

Write About The Walk:

_____
_____
_____
_____
_____
_____
_____
_____
_____
_____
_____
_____
_____
_____
_____
_____
_____
_____
_____
_____
_____
_____
_____
_____
_____
_____
_____
_____
_____
_____
_____

Rate Your Walk:

<u>Spectacular</u>   <u>Terrible</u>

1   2   3   4   5

Would You Go On This Walk Again & Why?:

_____
_____
_____
_____
_____
_____
_____
_____
_____
_____
_____
_____
_____
_____
_____
_____
_____

A Walk To Remember

Date: _____

Location: _____

Weather: _____

Company:

_____
_____
_____

Key Memorable Moments:

_____
_____
_____
_____
_____
_____
_____

Write About The Walk:

_____

_____

_____

_____

_____

_____

_____

_____

_____

_____

_____

_____

_____

_____

_____

_____

_____

_____

_____

_____

_____

_____

_____

_____

_____

_____

_____

_____

_____

_____

Rate Your Walk:

Spectacular   Terrible

1   2   3   4   5

Would You Go On This Walk Again & Why?:

_____
_____
_____
_____
_____
_____
_____
_____
_____
_____
_____
_____
_____
_____
_____
_____
_____

A Walk To Remember

Date: _____

Location: _____

Weather: _____

Company:

_____
_____
_____

Key Memorable Moments:

_____
_____
_____
_____
_____
_____
_____

Write About The Walk:

_____

_____

_____

_____

_____

_____

_____

_____

_____

_____

_____

_____

_____

_____

_____

_____

_____

_____

_____

_____

_____

_____

_____

_____

_____

_____

_____

_____

_____

Rate Your Walk:

<u>Spectacular</u>   <u>Terrible</u>

1   2   3   4   5

Would You Go On This Walk Again & Why?:

_____
_____
_____
_____
_____
_____
_____
_____
_____
_____
_____
_____
_____
_____
_____
_____

A Walk To Remember

Date: _____

Location: _____

Weather: _____

Company:

_____
_____
_____

Key Memorable Moments:

_____
_____
_____
_____
_____
_____
_____

Write About The Walk:

_____
_____
_____
_____
_____
_____
_____
_____
_____
_____
_____
_____
_____
_____
_____
_____
_____
_____
_____
_____
_____
_____
_____
_____
_____
_____
_____
_____
_____

Rate Your Walk:

Spectacular   Terrible

1   2   3   4   5

Would You Go On This Walk Again & Why?:

_____
_____
_____
_____
_____
_____
_____
_____
_____
_____
_____
_____
_____
_____
_____
_____
_____

About The Author

Born in Scotland, United Kingdom, Stacey Lannigan has always had a passion for creating and writing stories. She currently lives in Glasgow, Scotland, works as a full-time administrative assistant for a building contractor, owns her own professional freelance business: 'Lannigan Freelance Services', studies English Literature & Creative Writing through the Open University, and is a published author as of September 2021. In her free time, Stacey enjoys writing, reading, watching movies & tv shows, and spending time with her beloved cat, Weasley.

Did You Know?

Did you know that you can keep up to date with all of Stacey Lannigan's latest works and activity by subscribing to her website (*https://www.lanniganfreelanceservices.com*) or following her on Instagram at: *lanniganfreelanceservices*.

Printed in Great Britain
by Amazon